# The Men Behind the Flying Saucer Review

## By Steve Holland & Roger Perry

Published for Bear Alley Books by Createspace, 2017

http://bearalleybooks.blogspot.co.uk/

Copyright © Steve Holland & Roger Perry 2013

# Foreword

'The Men Behind the Flying Saucer Review' arose out of discussions I had with its co-author, Roger Perry, about writer and editor Charles Bowen. Roger had very kindly taken some time to interview his former colleague Dan Lloyd, the results of which were published on my Bear Alley blog in September 2013. Knowing Dan's connections with the *Flying Saucer Review*, I was interested in learning more about the *FSR's* former editor, Charles Bowen, who contributed features to *Boys' World*, a boys' comic which Roger had worked on and which I was writing about at the time; the resulting book was published in September 2013. Roger also knew Bowen's name from his time on *Countdown*, where Roger was art editor and Bowen a contributor. It was our successful collaboration on this lengthy feature that led me to writing up the history of *Countdown* soon after, the finished book appearing in July 2014.

Information on Bowen proved to be a little elusive but his career provided a fascinating thread through the publishing history of the *Flying Saucer Review / FSR*, and we used this thread to take a look at some of the other people who helped put together the magazine, the first magazine of its kind to study the phenomenon of unidentified flying objects (UFOs) in a serious and objective way.

So, while we started out with simple intentions, centred around expanding our knowledge of the extraordinarily competent Charles Bowen, we found ourselves exploring the lives of other people key to the creation of *Flying Saucer Review* until the results of what proved to be a fascinating journey through the magazine's history were presented in a 12-part serial published between 14 October to 3 November 2013.

Sadly, Roger passed away in 2016. I miss the critical back-and-forth of our e-mails as we argued over what should and should not be included in the series – a rather odd situation as both of us were of the "everything including the kitchen sink" school of writing. I have made only a few additions where new information has come to light and some minor changes for clarity to the original series and respectfully dedicate this e-book version to Roger's memory.

**Steve Holland**, 2017

# CHAPTER ONE: CHARLES BOWEN

Charles Arthur Bowen was born in St. Olave, Bermondsey, London, on Saturday, 21 September 1918. His father, Charles Frederick Bowen (1891-1977), had married Annie Gurden (1892-1970) at St. Anne's Church, Bermondsey, on 29 July 1915 and over the next few years had four children. Charles senior's father, Charles Richard Bowen (1861-1945), had been an artistic print colourist living in south London districts of Camberwell and Lambeth. The last publicly available census records (1911) reveal that Charles Frederick Bowen, the fifth of ten children, was still living in the family home – then at 74 Patmos Road in North Brixton – and was working as a clerk for the Manchester Book Cloth Co. The 17-year-old Charles had joined the territorial army and served four years with the 21st Battalion London Regiment until 1913.

Other than that he grew up in the Wandsworth area of London, little is known about Charles Bowen's early life. He had three younger siblings, of whom brother Derek died as a child. His sisters, twins Marjorie and Olive, were ten years younger and were evacuated at the outbreak of the Second World War. Bowen was serving in Norway with the Welsh Fusiliers when it fell to the Germans, and his family, whose London home had been destroyed by German bombs, heard nothing for a while. The appearance of a young telegraph boy at their door did nothing to quell their fears until the telegram was read: "In Scotland. Broke. Please wire £5". Bowen also served in Sierra Leone and rose to the rank of Staff Sergeant in Intelligence, working on radio and radar.

Bowen had married Helen Williams in November 1940 and a son, Michael, was born in 1942. She spent part of the war in Chichester with in-laws after an unexploded bomb under her London home sent her seeking alternative accommodation. Bowen eventually had four children, including Pauline, born in 1948, who in adult life became a competent artist, following in her mother's artistic footsteps.

For his remaining working life, Bowen was employed as a cashier in the Finance Department of the South African Embassy. It is likely, therefore, that at some point, he must have had some form of training as an accountant.

Sitting in front of his accounts books, it appears that Bowen's major interest outside of work was as a feature writer. It is not known when he began putting pen to paper but, during the 1950s, a variety of sporting articles began appearing in the popular boys' comic *Eagle*.

Aside from writing, Bowen had a growing fascination for gathering everything he possibly could on a phenomenon that was creeping into newspapers—UFO sightings. The most widely-known of these curious incidents was the alleged crash-landing of an alien craft in 1947 near Roswell in New Mexico. It's supposed concealment ultimately generated a mini-industry of publications suggesting a government cover-up.

But it was another strange, unearthly happening at around that same time but closer to home that was the catalyst in unearthing Bowen's ultimately long-lasting interest. This was the ten-month long mystery of what became known as "Ghost Rockets". Although first seen on February 26th by Finnish observers, these "ghost rockets" were witnessed mainly over Sweden and several neighbouring countries between May and December of 1946. Around 2,000 sightings were logged (about 10% having been confirmed by RADAR) with peaks of activity on the 9th and 11th of August. It was further claimed that authorities had been able to recover physical fragments that were attributed to these "ghost rockets".

Investigation concluded that many sightings were probably meteors, especially those on the 9th to 11th August as this coincided with the annual peak of the Perseid meteor shower. However, most sightings occurred outside of this precisely-scheduled meteor shower and the "ghost rockets" did not display the normal characteristics of a falling meteor.

Even at this early stage, Bowens' belief was that these visitors were not from an alien world ... but were possibly from a parallel dimension.

# CHAPTER TWO: DEREK DEMPSTER

Born in Tangier, Morocco, on 12 November 1924, Derek David Dempster was the youngest of three children born to Ernest Dempster, policy advisor on Moroccan affairs to the US Government, and his wife Bessie Ada Louise Dempster. His elder siblings were Joyce Celmenoda Dempster and Fergus Lee Dempster (OBE, DSC). He was educated, initially, at the French Lycee Regnault in northern Tangier but completed his schooling in England by attending Framlingham College (1938-40), St Edwards, (1940-42) and Pembroke College, Cambridge, (1942-43).

In 1943, Dempster joined the Royal Air Force and was sent off to Southern Rhodesia for pilot training. On gaining a commission and receiving his 'wings', he volunteered for the Fleet Air Arm in Middlesex, remaining there until he was demobbed in 1947. Thereafter he returned to Pembroke where he earned a BA in Law in 1947 and an MA in 1949.

In 1948 Dempster became a test pilot in the first age of British jet aircraft, joining 604 Squadron, based at North Weald in Epping Forest, Essex.

He initially flew Vampires, later moving onto Gloster Meteors – an innovative development in fighter planes that relied heavily on ground-breaking turbo-jet engines developed by Sir Frank Whittle. Flight-Lieutenant Dempster was chosen to attempt a 1,500-mile record flight from England to Casablanca in a light plane during the summer of 1954. Unfortunately, Dempster, at 14 stone, was considered too heavy for the task and he was replaced by 9-stone John Lee of the same squadron.

It was during Dempster's time at North Weald that an incident involving Flight Lieutenant James R Slandin had occurred and one that was immediately classified as being nothing short of Top Secret. It had happened on Thursday, 14 October 1954. There are a number of variants to Flt Lt Slandin's account of what happened on the day he flew over the seaside town of Southend. The following is taken from a 1985 interview conducted by ufologist Timothy Good for his book *Above Top Secret: The Worldwide UFO Cover-up* (1987):

> When I was at about 16,000 feet I saw a whole lot of contrails – possibly at 30-40,000 feet-over the North Foreland. Through the middle of the trails I saw three objects which I thought were airplanes, but they weren't

trailing. They came down through the middle of that toward Southend and then headed toward me.

When they got to within a certain distance two of them went off to my port side – one gold and one silver – and the third object came straight toward me and closed to within a few hundred yards, almost filling the windscreen, then it went off toward my port side. I tried to turn round to follow, but it had gone.

It was saucer-shaped with a bun on top and a bun underneath, and was silvery and metallic. There were no portholes, flames, or anything.

Slandin immediately reported the sighting by radio to the control tower at North Weald, continues Good in his book. "After landing he related further details to Derek Dempster, 604 Squadron's intelligence officer (sic) . . . The report was sent to the Air Ministry but nothing further was heard about it. Had it not been for Derek Dempster, the story might never have come to light." (Good's summary is quoted in full at http://www.nicap.org/reports/541004essex_good.htm.)

During his time as a test pilot, Dempster had written articles for Reuters and *The Airplane* magazine and, in the early-1950s, he had taken on the job as air correspondent with the *Daily Express*. It was through the Express that he was asked to review the book *Flying Saucers Have Landed* by Desmond Leslie and George Adamski, published by T. Werner Laurie in the late summer of 1953.

This was a hugely popular book, selling over 50,000 copies in eight editions in its first year, and had generated a great deal of discussion in the media, including a BBC North radio programme in December 1953 involving co-author Desmond Leslie and astronomer Professor Lovell.

Soon after, Dempster was dropped by the *Express* after he took a stand against Lord Beaverbrook, the paper's owner, who wanted him to condemn BOAC for grounding the Comet after it had suffered two fatal accidents in early 1954—an action Dempster supported.

This state of unemployment conveniently coincided with the imminent birth of a magazine called the *Flying Saucer Review*. Within a very short space of time of meeting one of the principals behind the publication of Leslie and Adamski's book, Dempster found himself installed in an office at T Werner Laurie in Doughty Street, London, as the first editor of *Flying Saucer Review*.

In later years, Dempster's own literary output included *The Tale of the Comet* and *The Narrow Margin* (co-written with Derek Wood), which served as a prime source for the making of Guy Hamilton's 1969 film *Battle of Britain* starring Michael Caine, Laurence Olivier, and Christopher Plummer. He was the director of a number of companies, including Debate Aviation Safety Ltd., Q. Publications Ltd., Aviation Study Group and The Quiet Pint Ltd. as Author, Consultant, Director and Publisher.

He died on 25 January 2012 aged 87. He married Isolde Ustinow (*née* Denham, 1920-1987), the former wife of actor Peter Ustinov, in 1951 and became stepfather to their daughter, Tamara. They subsequently divorced and he married Josephine Carole Newton in 1968.

## PUBLICATIONS BY DEREK DEMPSTER

**Non-fiction**
*The Inhabited Universe. An Inquiry into the Frontiers of Knowledge*, with Kenneth W. Gatland. London, Allan Wingate, 1957; New York, David McKay Co., 1958; as *Worlds In Creation*, Chicago, Henry Regnery, 1974.
*The Tale of the Comet*. London, Allan Wingate, 1959.
*The Narrow Margin*, with Derek Wood. London, Hutchinson, 1961; New York, McGraw-Hill Book Co., 1961; revised as *A Summer for Heroes*, Shrewsbury, Airlife, 1990.
*The Frontiers of Knowledge*, with Kenneth Gatland. London, Allan Wingate, 1974.
*The Quiet Pint: A Guide to Quiet Pubs*, with Josephine Dempster. Sandwich, "Q" Publications, 1995; 2nd ed. Sandwich, Q, 1996; 3rd ed. 1998; 4th ed. London, Aurum, 2000; 6th ed. London, Aurum, 2004.

# CHAPTER THREE: WAVENEY GIRVAN

Ian Waveney Girvan was born in London, in 1908, although at the time of the 1911 census he was in the charge of his grandfather and the care of a German nurse named Rosa Schurr. His grandfather, Alfred Woods of Ingate Lodge, Beccles, Wangford, Suffolk, was a 74-year-old, retired Court dressmaker, born in Lowestoft.

His father was Alexander Girvan, F.R.C.S., M.D., a Scotsman born in Maybole, Ayrshire, on 5 December 1871, the son of Robert Girvan, a GP. Alec (as he signed himself in the 1911 census) was a captain in the R.A.M.C. (Royal Army Medical Corps) who was married in 1904 to Alfred Woods' daughter, 39-year-old Delia Ellen Woods. The family home was at 8 Palace Street, Buckingham Gate, S.W., which is probably where Ian Waveney Girvan was born, as his birth is registered at nearby St George Hanover Square.

Delia was six years her husband's elder and already in her early forties when her son was born. She died, aged only 52, on 2 May 1917. Captain Alexander Girvan relinquished his commission on 9 April 1922.

Waveney Girvan was educated at Shewsbury School and then trained as an accountant. He developed an early interest in literature and penned a bibliography of the works of Henry Williamson (author of *Tarka the Otter*), which led to some correspondence with an American collector, H. Spafford Moore of Germanstown, Philadelphia. Two letters from 1931 offer a little insight into Girvan and his life.

The first (dated 4 May 1931) has the address 54 Brooke Road West, Waterloo, nr. Liverpool, and Girvan notes that he has just returned from a holiday which ended up in Belgium. However, the most interesting section discusses his love of Devon:

> Devon certainly is a glorious country and were I to give a visitor the best impression of these islands I should take him to Devon. I am a Scotch man (or should it be Scotsman) and I can be pardoned for boasting about it. I think it is the variety and richness of its scenery that places it above all others. It has wild highlands in Dartmoor and Exmoor. In Dartmoor the land rises to 2,000 feet above sea-level 'which is not bad for a

temperate isle' as Mr. Arnold Bennett once said. Exmoor sweeps down to the sea in heather-covered slopes and bare precipices. In the south are the attractive red-coloured cliffs and pleasant, well wooded with the good red earth. Her rivers the Dart, Teign, Tamar, Plym and many others are noted for their beauty. But the mind as well as the eye is attracted for Devon is also famed for her men and associations. And she can boast of a literature that is growing in importance. It is wealthy in superstitions, folk-lore and old survivals. Perhaps you can forgive my eulogies. I spent the happiest years of my life in Devon and Cornwall and regard myself as an exile.

A second, undated letter, later but probably not long after, has the address 5 Corfton Road, Ealing W.5. and begins "Your letter has been forwarded to me. I now work in the city of London and earn my living as a tutor in Accountancy." Later in the same letter he notes "I find living in London very expensive and I have had to curtail my book-buying to a certain extent. But I shall recover."

An Associate of the Institute of Chartered Accountants (A.C.A.), he continued to work as an accountant throughout the 1930s whilst living at a number of addresses: in 1933-36 he was at 12 Ilkenham Close, Ruislip, Middlesex; in 1937-38, the London phone book gives his address as Shilla The Village, Denham, then Tudor Lodge, Denham Village from 1939, at which address he remained until at least 1956. As an accountant – a protected industry – he was not conscripted during the Second World War; instead, he was employed as an accountant by Security Steel Strappings of Sheffield.

There was also a political aspect to his distance from the fighting forces. Girvan became involved with the organisation of the Parliamentary Peace Aims Group, set up in 1939 to promote a negotiated peace with Hitler; he was investigated by the police in 1940 for defeatist and subversive comments.

Girvan was involved in the set-up of Westaway Books Ltd., based at Tudor House, Princeton Street, London W.C.1, in 1948, who published books dedicated to the west country. His colleagues included J. C. Trewin OBE (1908-1990), formerly a journalist on the Western Independent, who edited *West Country Magazine* for the company. His co-director was former MP and one-time Director of Publications of the British Union of Fascists (editing *Action* and *Blackshirt*), John Warburton Beckett. The company was financed by Hastings William Sackville Russell, the Duke of Bedford.

Girvan knew Beckett and Russell (then Lord Tavistock; he succeeded to the title Duke of Bedford in 1940) through his involvement with the British People's Party (BPP), an anti-war party founded by Beckett and Lord Tavistock after Beckett split with the National Socialist League in 1939 – shortly before his N.S.L. ally William "Lord Haw-Haw" Joyce fled to Germany to become a Nazi propaganda broadcaster. The BPP was not proscribed during the war because of its titled patron; Beckett, on the other hand, was interred for the duration. Girvan was also involved with other organisations during this period, including the National Front and Independent Nationalists. The National Front, in this case, was the National Front After Victory, a group founded by A. K. Chesterton and briefly allied with the BPP, which drew the interest of people as diverse as philanthropist Viscount Nuffield, fascist Jeffrey Hamm, and author Henry Williamson (also a former member of Mosley's British Union of Fascists).

After the war, the BPP continued to exist until the Duke of Bedford's death in 1954.

During his time with Westaway Books, Girvan was also Chairman of the West Country Writers' Association, who shared the same Tudor House address as the publisher. The group was co-founded by Victor Bonham-Carter. Also based at Tudor House was a second publishing house, Carroll & Nicholson, which published a broader range of titles than Westaway, ranging from Hesketh Pearson's *A Life of Shakespeare* to popular crime titles *Oscar Slater: The Great Suspect* by Peter Hunt and *The Wallace Case* by John Rowland. Girvan joined the larger company, reputedly through the machinations of John Beckett, who hoped a friendlier editor would mean more right-leaning books.

One of Carroll & Nicholson's titles was *The Riddle of the Flying Saucers* by Gerald Heard. Girvan revealed the background to the book a few years later in *Flying Saucers and Common Sense*, in which he spoke about the development of his interest in UFOs:

> My first step in 1949 was to subscribe to a newspaper cutting agency to send me anything they could discover where the words 'flying saucer' were used. To begin with these cuttings were not numerous in England. I do not know whether it was because the incidents were few or whether, in England, the saucers had not then received the publicity that was later to be theirs. However, in 1949 and 1950 the cuttings produced some interesting evidence. Not that there was, at that time, anything very startling, but one was able to learn quite a lot about the human reactions. Most of my cuttings at that time came from local papers: the national papers did not then pay much attention to the subject...
>
> The Spring of 1950 produced quite a good crop over this country, but it was quite over-shadowed by the mass of sightings that were being reported over the United States. It was at this time that the opinion grew that it was American mass-hysteria that was responsible. It was quite extraordinary how the English sightings, though they were comparatively few, were being ignored. My cuttings still arrived but they were for the most part, from local and not national papers.

With interest growing, Girvan commissioned a book on the subject from Gerald Heard (Henry FitzGerald Heard, 1889-1971), who produced *The Riddle of the Flying Saucers*, serialised in the *Sunday Express* in October 1950. It was subsequently published by Carroll & Nicholson in the UK and as *Is Another World Watching?* in America.

The *Sunday Express* was, at the time, in a circulation battle with the *Sunday Dispatch*, and flying saucers were a topic that helped boost sales. Charles Eade, editor of the *Sunday Dispatch*, had been alerted to their potential by Lord Mountbatten, and ran extracts from *Flying Saucers Are Real* (Hutchinson, 1950) by Donald Keyhoe and *Behind the Flying Saucers* by Frank Scully (Gollancz, 1950). With public interest booming, Britain's Chief Scientific Advisor, Sir Henry Tizard, set up the Flying Saucer Working Party at the Ministry of Defence to investigate reports of future sightings.

George Greenfield, who in 1952 was looking for a successor as editor at T. Werner Laurie, recalled in his memoir *A Smattering of Monsters*:

A youngish, dark-haired Cornishman *(sic)* with glowing eyes named Waveney Girvan was a member of the Authors' Club. He was a publisher, in charge of a small firm named Westaway Books, owned by the then Duke of Bedford ... He was, according to Girvan, wildly eccentric and although enormously wealthy – he owned most of the area between Tottenham Court Road and Southampton Row, apart from the vast family seat at Woburn – he was parsimonious, insisting on keeping a close, almost daily, watch on his publishing venture, even though it accounted for a minute part of his income. The Cornish are themselves a strange breed, as I know from having had a Cornish grandmother, a Waveney Girvan, I soon discovered, believed in UFOs and visitations from other planets. But he had more than met his match in His Grace, *le patron*, whose ideas for likely publications were far weirder than his own. In short, he was fed up.

    Luckily for me, he unburdened himself over a bottle of wine at the club just as I had come to a cul-de-sac in my thoughts for a successor. I tried not to paint too rosy a picture of life at Number One, Doughty Street – I was fond of my colleagues and of many authors I would be leaving behind – but I may have glossed over the amount of interference he was likely to get from the other watchdog directors. At least, none of them was, in the modern jargon, barking mad, like his present owner. ("Pray tell me, sir, whose dog are you?")

    And so it came to pass. His *curriculum vitae* impressed Herbert Rothbarth, and the other directors of Werner Laurie took to him at the following interview. I absented myself, having an interest to declare, but it must have been so, as they promptly offered him the succession. He was able to serve out his notice at Westaway Books and spend a few days taking over in time for me – after six years to the very day – to say goodbye to publishing and jump over the fence into the new world of ten per cent.

Girvan arrival at T. Werner Laurie coincided with the arrival of a manuscript from a member of the Anglo-Irish aristocracy, Desmond Leslie (1921-2001). While he was touting his book around various publishers, Leslie heard of a Polish-born American, George Adamski, who claimed to have photographed alien spaceships in the Californian skies and who later, in 1952, said he was taken on a trip to Venus by an alien visitor to Earth. Leslie contacted Adamski who sent him copies of his photographs and then sent him a manuscript detailing his adventures. Leslie submitted both his and Adamski's manuscripts to Werner Laurie and Waveney Girvan suggested that the two were combined in a single book.

## PUBLICATIONS BY WAVENEY GIRVAN

### Non-fiction
*A Bibliography and a Critical Survey of the Works of Henry Williamson* by I. Waveney Girvan, together with authentic bibliographical annotations by another hand. Chipping Campden, Gloucestershire, Alcuin Press, 1931.
*Eden Phillpotts: An Assessment and a Tribute.* London, Hutchinson, 1953.
*Flying Saucers and Common Sense.* London, Frederick Muller, 1955.

### Others
*Amaryllis at the Fair* by John Jefferies, with an introduction by Waveney Girvan. London, Westaway Books, 1948.

# CHAPTER FOUR: DESMOND LESLIE

According to his obituary in the *Daily Telegraph*, "The prevailing scientific materialism of Leslie's time held no appeal to him, and he turned his attention instead to the world of mysteries. Attracted to ancient history, archaeology and esoteric philosophy, he saw in them evidence of a world view quite different from that of more soberly academic contemporaries. To Leslie, ancient monuments and artefacts were proof of a sophistication of culture and technology that could not be attributed to the people of their times. The makers, he concluded, were evidently super-human—or came from elsewhere. In the 1950s, there were regular reports of "flying saucers" and of encounters with alien creatures, and Leslie's merger of these accounts with his antiquarian researches led to *The Flying Saucers Have Landed*."

The latter, described as "a key text of the New Age movement", was jointly credited to George Adamski, a Polish-born American who developed an interest in Eastern religions in the 1930s, founding a group known as the Royal Order of Tibet. In 1952, Adamski claimed that he was invited aboard a flying saucer and taken to Venus.

Aliens from Venus is a key element of Theosophy, which Leslie used as one of the bases for his book, which consisted of his own main section (Book One), taking up over three-quarters of the volume, with the shorter Adamski manuscript (Book Two) attached. Leslie's foreword opens as follows: "About eighteen million years ago, say the strange and ancient legends of our little planet" before citing a number of books written by Theosophists—Alice Bailey, Annie Besant, H. P. Blavatsky and C. W. Leadbeater.

Central to Leslie's book was Sanat Kumara who, according to Blavetsky, belonged to a group of beings known as the Lords of the Flame. This theme was developed by Leadbeater and Bailey. Wikipedia notes: "C.W. Leadbeater and later adherents of Theosophy such as Alice A. Bailey believe that Sanat Kumara came to Earth 18,500,000 years ago (A.E. Powell gives a figure of 16,500,000 years ago) from the etheric plane of the planet Venus ... In Theosophy, the beings that helped Sanat Kumara organize the expedition from Venus are called the "Lords of the Flame"."

Mix in numerous reports from newspapers and magazines and Leslie's book alone might have made an interesting read. However, as Charles

Davy noted in *The Observer* (4 October 1953): "Mr. Desmond Leslie's diligent but wildly speculative inquiries into the ancient history of flying saucers are overshadowed by Mr. George Adamski's story of the present day."

Even the book's editor had problems with the story, Charles Bowen later recalled (*FSR* v.16 no.3, 1970): "When it appeared in September 1953, the book had obviously benefited from Waveney Girvan's editing skill—during our years of close association he told me of the difficulties he had faced, and how he overcame them." Sadly, Bowen never expanded on the topic. Bowen does, however, discuss the reaction to the book's appearance:

> A predictable blast effect was the instant raising of the voices of protest among reviewers. The general implication was that Adamski was a liar, a cheat and a hoaxer; others, later, thought he may have been hoaxed by someone else. Some, more charitable, were of the opinion that Adamski had seen, and photographed, a strange aerial object, and that he had suffered an hallucination which gave rise to the sensational story he told.
> An unpredictable blast effect was the enthusiasm with which the public rushed to buy the book, in spite of the reviews. Another effect was the way a "contactee" cult sprang into being around the person of George Adamski, an effect which, according to some, has done more damage to the possibility of serious research on UFOs than could have resulted from the pontifications of a thousand Menzels! While this may be true, it is equally true that many thousands of reasonable people first met the subject through the agency of this book, and thereafter decided, in a rational way, to find out more about UFOs. These people did not join the ranks of the vehement protesters, and they did not become cultists. In fact many of them eventually became readers of *Flying Saucer Review*, for another of the effects of the dynamite blast was the founding of this journal late in 1954 by Waveney Girvan and a handful of friends.
> The success of the Leslie / Adamski book prompted these dedicated people to think the time was ripe for establishing a serious journal on the subject. (This is

contrary to a view sometimes expressed that the *FSR* was founded to disseminate the cultist beliefs of the "contactees" and their followers.)

Even Bowen, who believed in UFOs, thought the Adamski story damaged serious research as it was "seemingly ridiculous" and "makes the subject laughable". However he retains his ire for Adamski's followers: "I have long felt that although the story seems ridiculous, and the chief witness created a poor impression of himself, the greatest danger to the subject lay in the subsequent cultism. The story itself is no more "ridiculous" than the bulk of the contact stories."

Leslie stood by Adamski and claimed that, on a visit to Adamski in California in 1954, he had seen
several flying saucers. Back in the UK, he teamed up with Brinsley le Poer Trench and helped with the creation of the *Flying Saucer Review*.

Leslie subsequently revised and expanded the book in 1970, but it has been largely forgotten by anyone outside the UFO community.

Leslie himself was also a somewhat forgotten character. Almost any mention of him tells us that he was an Irish aristocrat, who made the front pages in 1963 when he punched Bernard Levin live on *That Was The Week That Was* after the critic slated his wife's first solo show, *Cabaret of Savagery and Delight*, based on songs by Kurt Weill and Bertolt Brecht.

There is a question over quite where Leslie was born, with some sources saying he was born in Co. Monaghan, Ireland (Wikipedia [https://en.wikipedia.org/wiki/Desmond_Leslie] for instance), while other sources give London as his place of birth (including Contemporary Authors and travel records, from information supplied by Leslie himself). As Desmond A. Leslie, his birth was registered in Marylebone, London, in 3Q 1921.

He was born Desmond Arthur Peter Leslie on 29 June 1921, the son of Sir John Randolph Shane Leslie, the eccentric and colourful 3rd Baronet of Castle Leslie, Glaslough, Co. Monaghan. Shane Leslie had travelled widely and, alongside his political ambitions, was also an author. The family fortune waned following the Wall Street Crash but picked up in 2002 when Castle Leslie was the secret location of the marriage of Paul McCartney and Heather Mills.

Leslie studied at Ampleforth and Trinity College, Dublin, before joining the RAF during the Second World War, flying Spitfires and Hurricanes, destroying several planes (a family historian remarked that they were mostly those he was piloting). He celebrated VE day with his cousin, the Prime Minister, at 10 Downing Street.

In August 1945, he married Agnes Bernauer, the daughter of Rudolph Bernauer, a German Jewish impresario who had fled to London in 1936. In 1954, using her stage name Agnes Bernelle, she became the first actress to perform nude, as Salome at St Martin's Theatre, although her career developed as a singer as the decade moved on.

Leslie, meanwhile, worked in the film industry, writing and directing films, and as an author, his novels including *Careless Lives* (1945), *Pardon My Return* (1946) and *Angels Weep* (1946). Later novels included *Hold Back The Night* (1956), *The Amazing Mr. Lutterworth* (1958) and *The Jesus File* (1975). He was involved in the movies *My Hands Are Clay* (1947), *Stranger At My Door* (1950), *The Missing Princess* (1954, starring his wife) and *Them And The Thing* (1960).

During the shooting of *Stranger At My Door*, with money short, Leslie decided to create all the music himself. This interest in music developed, and he created a working multi-track sound mixing desk and, later, began recording experimental music, beginning with *Music Of The Future* in 1960 (although not commercially available until 2005). The track 'Mercury', for instance, was created using a spinning top and a horn from an old Morris Oxford. In the 1960s, he was involved with recording a series of Shakespeare plays in stereo performed by Old Vic players and released as 'The Living Shakespeare'. In the UK, the records were produced by Odhams. Some of his many recordings—bees humming, cars hooting, babies crying—were used as incidental music or soundtracks to TV shows.

In 1963, whilst expecting their third child, Leslie and his wife moved from London to Ireland and concentrated on rebuilding the fortunes of Castle Leslie, firstly through a club, Annabel's on the Bog (after the famous London nightclub, Annabel's). Guests included Mick Jagger, Marianne Faithful and Patrick Moore, but it did not last long. Moore later collaborated with Leslie on a spoof book, *How Britain Won The Space Race* (1972).

His marriage to Agnes was dissolved in 1969 and he subsequently married Helen Jennifer Strong, with whom he had two daughters. They moved to St. Jeannet in the South of France in the late 1980s, where Leslie worked on various books, including an unpublished autobiography. He died in Antibes, France, on 24 February 2001, survived by his second wife and six children, one of them from an affair.

**PUBLICATIONS BY DESMOND LESLIE**

**Novels**
*Careless Lives*. London, Macdonald & Co., 1945.
*Pardon My Return*. London, Macdonald & Co., 1946.
*Angels Weep*. London, T. Werner Laurie, 1946.
*Hold Back the Night*. London, P. Owen, 1956.
*The Amazing Mr. Lutterworth*. London, Wingate, 1958.

**Non-fiction**
*Flying Saucers Have Landed*, with George Adamski. London, British Book Center, 1953; revised and enlarged, London, Neville Spearman, 1970.
*How Britain Won the Space Race*, with Patrick Moore. London, Mitchell Beazley, 1972.
*True Horsemanship Through Feel*, with Bill Dorrance. Novato, CA, Diamond Lu Productions, 1999.

# CHAPTER FIVE: BRINSLEY LE POER TRENCH

Whilst Desmond Leslie was not one of the five players directly involved in the launch of *Flying Saucer Review*, his book was a key element in its launch. Another aristocrat, however, put his money where his mouth was and was one of the magazine's financial backers in its early days before taking over as editor.

Brinsley Le Poer Trench claimed he could trace his family origins back to around 63,000 B.C., when aliens landed on Earth. Other aliens ascended from below the surface of the planet from civilisations that still exist. "I haven't been down there myself," he later admitted, "but from what I gather [these civilisations] are very advanced." Adam and Eve, Noah and other biblical characters were from Mars, Trench believed.

On a more down-to-Earth level, his family tree can easily be traced back to Irish politician Frederick Richard Trench (1681-1752), his son Richard Trench, and grandson, William Power Keating Trench, who became the Earl of Clancarty, taking the name from a "tenuous link" to the Munster Earls of Clancarty. The 2nd Earl of Clancarty, Richard, was also made Marquess of Heusden in 1815 for his aid in resolving Dutch border disputes. Le Poer was an old noble Irish name dating back to the Norman invasion of Ireland.

William Francis Brinsley Le Poer Trench was the fifth son of William Fredrick Le Poer Trench, the 5th Earl of Clancarty, and inherited his titles following the deaths of two older brothers (Richard in 1971 and Greville in 1975), making him the 8th Earl of Clancarty and 7th Marquess of Heusden. (More information on the lineage can be found on Wikipedia [https://en.wikipedia.org/wiki/Earl_of_Clancarty].)

Trench was raised in London and educated at the Pangbourne Nautical College, and had taken up employment for a while selling advertising space for a gardening magazine whose offices were housed in a building opposite the Waterloo mainline Station. After the success of his first book, published in 1960, he was able to write full-time.

Trench's interest in UFOs had developed after the war and, finding others with similar interests, he was involved in the early years of the *Flying*

*Saucer Review*, selling advertising space and eventually taking over the editorship between 1956 and 1959. He also founded the International UFO Observer Corps in 1956, which had observers watching the skies until 1960 when it was closed down as few reports came in from members involved and some, having failed to sight a UFO, turned to other forms of evidence gathering—"mediumship, myths and traditions, leading to preconceived opinions inimical to research with open minds."

Trench served as vice-president of the The British UFO Research Association (BUFORA), founded in 1962. He was chairman of the International Committee of the International Sky Scouts, founded in 1965 and who held a flying saucer spotting day on 24 June 1966. The International Sky Scouts became Contact International in 1967 with Trench their first president; their newsletter – *Awareness* – became *Awareness: Journal of Contact*. He was also an honorary life member of the now defunct "Ancient Astronauts Society" which supported ideas that had been put forward by Erich von Däniken in his 1968 book *Chariots of the Gods?*.

In 1975 he succeeded to the earldom on the death of his half-brother thus entitling him to a seat in the British Parliament. He used his new position to found a UFO Study Group at the House of Lords, introduce the *Flying Saucer Review* magazine to its library and push for the declassification of UFO data.

Four years later he organised a celebrated debate in the House of Lords on UFOs which attracted many speeches on both sides of the question, with Lords Kimberley, Oxfuird, Davies of Leek and Cork speaking in Clancarty's support. In one debate, Lord Stabolgi, for the Government, declared that there was nothing to convince him that any alien spacecraft had ever visited the Earth. John Ezard reported Clancarty's response on another occasion when he was challenged to prove that aliens were on earth: "Well, you do see a lot of strange people about, don't you," replied Clancarty.

Lest it be thought that Lord Clancarty was simply using his privileged position to promote his own ideas, it should be noted that he also attended almost every meeting of the Lords defence group and was interested in services for the sick, the poor and the alcoholic. He was described by Lord Kimberley as "a terribly kind man".

Clancarty was married four times. He died in a nursing home in Bexhill-on-Sea, Sussex, on 18 May 1995, survived by his fourth wife. His titles passed to his nephew, Nicholas Le Poer Trench.

## PUBLICATIONS BY BRINSLEY LE POER TRENCH

**Non-fiction**
*The Sky People*. London, Neville Spearman, 1960.
*Men Among Mankind*. London, Neville Spearman, 1962, Amherst, WI, Amherst Press, 1963.
*Forgotten Heritage*. London, Neville Spearman, 1965.
*The Flying Saucer Story*. London, Neville Spearman, 1966.
*Operation Earth*. London, Neville Spearman, 1969.
*The Eternal Subject*. London, Souvenir Press, 1973, as *Mysterious Visitors: The UFO Story*, New York, Stein and Day, 1973, revised, London, Pan Books, 1975.
*Secret of the Ages: UFOs from Inside the Earth*. London, Souvenir Press, 1974.

# CHAPTER SIX: DENIS MONTGOMERY

Over the preceding pages, we have detailed the three leading characters in the story behind the *Flying Saucer Review*—four if you include Desmond Leslie and the impetus his book gave to the notion of setting up a place for the serious study of UFOs. But in practical terms the creation of the paper was the responsibility of Waveney Girvan, Derek Dempster and Brinsley Le Poer Trench.

But there is, in fact, a genuine fourth. At around twenty years old, he was not only the youngest of the group, but perhaps he was the most influential in the way that, through him, the lives of those around him had been considerably altered.

Denis Montgomery was born in a farmworkers' clinic on a tea estate in Kearsney, Natal, in South Africa in 1934, the son of an Irishman who had emigrated to and fought for Australia during the Great War and a mother whose family were mid-19th century colonial pioneers.

After serving three years in the Navy, Montgomery attended the University of Natal before emigrating to England to study librarianship. It was whilst employed as an assistant librarian at Southwark University—now the London South Bank University (LSBU), based near the South Bank of the River Thames from which it now takes its name—that he first became aware of the UFO phenomenon.

It was 1953 and the heyday of UFO sightings and Montgomery developed a growing fascination for what he later called [http://www.fsr.org.uk/fsrintroduction.html] "the concept of interplanetary travel and the new idealism of a universal brotherhood of intelligent life." Vast numbers of people from all walks of life claimed to have seen, or had some sort of contact with, beings from another world over the previous half-a-dozen years. Scraps of information and feedback or speculation resulting from these reports was everywhere, but it went unrecorded and was subsequently being lost. Montgomery felt that there ought to be some form of institute or library whereby all these scraps of useful information could be amassed into a single, well-ordered collection area where it could be catalogued and filed away properly.

Montgomery made contact with Waveney Girvan, meeting him at the offices of T. Werner Laurie where he put forward his ideas. Girvan –

heavily into the throws of writing his own book *Flying Saucers and Common Sense* – had also been considering the possibility of putting together a serious and trustworthy magazine. A magazine, if it was successfully launched, could support the institute that he wanted, Montgomery believed, and, in turn, that would give the magazine an authoritative platform. In addition to a popular magazine, which provided revenue, maybe a learned journal could follow.

A meeting was arranged. And it is to this meeting that we shall return in a few days' time for our next chapter.

# CHAPTER SEVEN: THE LAUNCH OF FLYING SAUCER REVIEW

As with any history that involves more than one person, there are conflicting versions of how *Flying Saucer Review* began. There are sketchy references to regular meetings having taken place during the latter half of 1954. According to Derek Dempster (in *FSR* v.51 no.2, Autumn 2006), "We held meetings at Westminster, Caxton Hall, near Scotland Yard." Caxton Hall, originally used as a Town Hall during the Second World War, had been used by the Ministry of Information as a venue for press conferences held by Winston Churchill and his ministers. In succeeding years, it became a popular register office for high society celebrities and for those who had required a civil marriage and was the regular home of bi-monthly comic marts during the 1970s and 1980s.

There are no details as to whether these meetings had taken place weekly or monthly, nor as to whom or how many enthusiasts had actually attended. There is mention though of two highly-placed allies:

"We believed these things were coming in from outer space, and we were trying to prove this with science. We had some allies, such as Peter Horsley, who had been Station Commander at North Weald and was then Equerry to Prince Philip. Also, we received collaboration from Henry Chinnery, who was Horsley's successor."

Squadron Leader Horsley had joined the Royal Household as an Extra Equerry in 1949, rising to Temporary Equerry to the Queen in 1952 and full-time Equerry to the Duke of Edinburgh in 1953, a role he retained until 1956. Squadron Leader Chinnery, in the RAF since 1941, replaced Lieutenant-Commander Michael Parker as the Duke's Air Equerry when the latter departed suddenly after separating from his wife.

Both Horsley and Chinnery were eager in keeping the Palace fully informed – particularly in light of Lord Louie Mountbatten's well-advertised personal interest in the subject of flying saucers. The Admiral of the Fleet was known to have kept several lever files containing collected newspaper reports, jotted notes and UFO photographs on the bridge so that he might show these off to visitors at times when he was at sea.

At the next Caxton Hall meeting, Waveney Girvan – having been thoroughly fired up from the ideas Denis Montgomery had floated only a matter of days before – had introduced his new friend, and then announced their combined thoughts about floating a bi-monthly magazine, the subject of which would be entirely devoted to UFO phenomena.

With mounting enthusiasm, Derek Dempster, Brinsley le Poer Trench, Oliver Moxon (former RAF fighter pilot, charter pilot, publisher and author) and Lewis Barton (managing editor of the illustrated magazine *This Week* and author of two books for T. Werner Laurie) had all approved of the idea and had agreed to put in a bit of cash. It was agreed that a limited company should be formed and that Derek Dempster would become the magazine's first editor – not as daunting a task as it might sound for he was already acting as editor for BOAC's monthly house magazine. Working out of No. 1 Doughty Street, Waveney Girvan would be on hand to assist in giving him all the necessary typesetting, repro house and printing contacts, and he would have the commercial expertise as offered by Lewis Barton. With everything agreed, they all adjourned to a nearby pub to celebrate.

Gordon Creighton later recalled (*FSR* v.39 no.2, 1994), "Meanwhile, on December 15, 1954, the "Founding Fathers" of FSR had held their first meeting at 4 Berners Street, London W.1. The participants were Waveney Girvan, Derek Dempster, Desmond Leslie, Benjamin Harrington, Oliver Moxon, Lewis Barton, Desmond Judge and Denis Montgomery. On November 12, 1954, the company Flying Saucer Service Limited had been registered at Companies House, based at the 1 Doughty Street, London W.C.1 address of T. Werner Laurie. "Anyone seeing this weird title must surely have thought that it was some sort of *cosmic minicab* firm!" Creighton joked. Montgomery, who was company secretary, later revealed that:
The company was named Flying Saucer Service Ltd in order to portray its role as something more than a magazine publisher. It was a firm intention that it would eventually provide a service to researchers and other publishers and interested bodies with co-ordinated information, and to investigate sightings and happenings. It was hoped that with improved financial viability the company might expand into other related commercial activities.
Volume 1 Number 1 of *Flying Saucer Review*, although dated Spring, appeared in January 1955 and had a startling diagrammatic cover by Castle. For its first 83 issues (until v.14 no.6, 1968), the cover title was

*Flying Saucer Review* in full. The magazine was bold, unashamed and enthusiastic about its subject matter; Derek Dempster, the editor, set the tone on page one:

> [Flying Saucer Review]'s aim is to obtain and analyse as many reports and photographs as possible and to publish those considered authentic and important. Unpublished accounts and pictures analysed will be classified and filed for reference purposes.

This could almost be Denis Montgomery's vision come to life.

Beyond Dempster's editorial, there was an interview with Flight-Lieutenant J. R. Salandin, whose encounter with two circular objects in 1954 has been previously mentioned. Articles appeared signed by W. J. Brown, Leonard Cramp, John Rowland (described as "a recent convert to belief in flying saucers"), "Pisces" ("a prominent astronomer, who does not believe in flying saucers") and The Hon. Brinsley Le Poer Trench.

Leonard George Cramp (1919-2006) was a British aerospace engineer whose *Space, Gravity and the Flying Saucer*, published by T. Werner Laurie in 1954, looked at the engineering possibilities of flying saucers and included orthographic projections of flying saucer photographs and technical drawings of other UFOs.

Gordon Creighton, a foreign diplomat from the Ministry of Defence, recalls seeing proposals to publish a journal about Flying Saucers reported in London newspapers.

> I was back in England [by] then, and I made contact at once and received the subscription form from Brinsley le Poer Trench, later Lord Clancarty. My knowledge of a number of languages gave me the opportunity to begin contributing straight away, and my first [translated] piece appearing in the second issue of FSR (May/June 1955).

Creighton would play a most important part in the *Flying Saucer Review* story and deserves a closer look.

He was born Gordon William Creighton in Rickmansworth, Hertfordshire, on 26 April 1908, the son of William Creighton Jr., a Scottish-born travelling salesman who lived with his father, a farmer, at Piper's Farm, Rickmansworth, and his wife Mabel (nee Maloney). William and Mabel's marriage was brief and they divorced in January 1913 (William was later married again, in 1933, to Doris Storey).

Paul Whitehead, in an obituary for Creighton [http://ufoupdateslist.com/2003/jul/m19-005.shtml], said:

> He ran around barefoot for a few years, on the farm – with his grandfather standing in for his parents. He used to drink milk straight from cows – which is how he contracted tuberculosis. His friend died from the disease, but Gordon survived after an operation.
> When he did eventually go to school (age 11?), it was discovered that he had a bent for being multilingual and academic. This combination led him to a career in the diplomatic service, with elements of the secret service thrown in.

Creighton's late start did not prevent what *The Times* (16 August 2003) called "a conventional education" at Bishop's Stortford College, Cambridge University and the École Libre des Sciences Politiques in Paris.

His first posting was as an attaché to the British Embassy in Beijing. He subsequently served as H.M. Vice-Consul at Tientsin and H.M. Vice-Consul at Chungking before becoming First Secretary at Beijing. Further posts included periods in the Far Eastern Department of the Foreign Office in London, then as H.M. Consul at Nanking and at Shanghai. In Shanghai he survived the shelling by the Japanese at the outset of the Sino-Japanese War in 1937. Creighton, like many embassy staff, moved to Chungking, the Chinese provisional capital, and was stationed there during the early 1940s.

When he eventually returned to the UK, he had two very fortunate escapes, as recalled by Paul Whitehead:

> He had to leave China, and went to Sydney. A ship that he was due to leave on for England (but didn't) sank *en route* – sunk by the Germans . . . He instead caught a

boat that sailed east from Sydney to South America. This sailed up the east coast of South America; Gordon had to disembark (in Brazil, I think) and was airlifted to the US because he was very ill. In a storm, the ship that he had been on broke up, with large or total loss of life.

After World War II, in 1947, Creighton married Joan Karthlyn Felice Dudley (1922-1997) before taking up a post as H.M. Consul at Recife, Brazil, where his wife gave birth to twins, Philip Gordon William and Rosamund Lilian Margaret, in December 1948. The family returned to the UK when the twins were 15 months old.

After spells as Consul-General at Antwerp, Belgium, and New Orleans, USA, Creighton researched maps in oriental and other languages with the Permanent Committee on Geographical Names. His work was aided by his talent for languages; he studied twenty, including Chinese, Sanskrit, Tibetan, Mongolian, Burmese, Arabic and Russian.

He then spent eight years as an intelligence officer on Russian and Chinese affairs at the Ministry of Defence. He reputedly worked directly below the top secret department at Whitehall where the Air Ministry and RAF studied UFOs. This was a subject Creighton had become interested in during the summer of 1941 when he saw what he described as "a white disc with a piercingly bright bluish light on top racing through the sky in the far west of China near the eastern marches of Tibet".

Not that he liked the phrase "UFO", which he thought a monstrous term, deliberately introduced by American authorities, that was meekly accepted by American civilian researchers, followed by "all the others, like a flock of sheep".

"Flying Saucers" as a term also had its own problems and Creighton recorded (*FSR* v.39 no.2, 1994):

> [I]t was not long before we began to find that quite a lot of our readers – particularly the native Brits, who are well known for their traditional nervousness about "what the neighbours might think" – showed distinct squeamishness about signing cheques made out to "FLYING SAUCER REVIEW". Evidently they were pretty concerned about what their bank-manager might

> think of such politically incorrect behaviour! So, in the summer of 1971, I persuaded the other Directors that we should apply to the Registrar of Companies for our name to be switched from the ridiculous "FLYING SAUCER SERVICE LTD.", to "FSR PUBLICATIONS LTD." The bank-managers wouldn't have a clue as to what *that* meant, and would-be readers of FSR need no longer hang their heads in shame.

Creighton had no shame about what his neighbours thought. *The Times* noted:

> For 30 years, commuting daily from Hertfordshire to London, he "made a special point of carrying and reading *FSR* in the train up to Baker Street and then on the Underground". He was pleased to recall that "it must have happened on at least a dozen occasions that complete strangers would step across the gangway to me and say: "*Flying Saucer Review!* Where can I get that?"

*The Flying Saucer Review* continued to appear on a quarterly and then bi-monthly schedule. Using Waveney Girvan's contacts, the paper was produced efficiently and economically. The general harmony and enthusiasm of the group – plus the unstilted provision of individuals' time and energy – became a pleasurable memory. Nobody ever talked about remuneration.

There were, however, still many moments of difficulty to face over the years. One major problem was that in their attempt to give serious thought and study to the subject of UFOs and to collate as much information as they could, the paper was also covering the claims of hoaxers and the deluded.

"I met George Adamski at this time," recalled Derek Dempster many years later (*FSR* v.56 no.3, 2006). "I could see how terribly keen everybody was to embrace people like him who claimed he had travelled to Venus. I was less sure of him, and wished to remain objective. What we were all living on then was hope and expectation."

Adamski, whom Desmond Leslie had visited in 1954, published a follow-up to *Flying Saucers Have Landed* in 1955. Entitled *Inside the Space*

*Ships*, it detailed his trips around the solar system with, amongst others, Orthon the Venusian, a Martian named Firkon and Ramu the Saturnian. The book carried an introduction by Leslie.

Derek Dempster remained in the position as editor of *Flying Saucer Review* until the position became untenable in 1956. "We kept being shot down due to the activities of the lunatic fringe, who began to attach themselves to ufology. I had to leave FSR because of the effect it had on my business interests in the aviation industry; apart from that, I was being regarded as a 'nutcase', whose opinion in aviation matters was in question."

Dempster continued to work in the aviation industry, remaining a Flight-Lieutenant in the Royal Auxiliary Air Force until 1956. At the same time he was editor of the B.O.A.C. aircrew magazine and the weekly *B.O.A.C. News*, a position he retained until 1959. He continued to work in publishing (as Skylink Ltd. he published *Skytrader International*) and as an advisor and consultant through a number of firms including Economic Liaison Services, Airport Publishing Co., and Interface Publishing Consultants.

He continued to have an interest in UFOs and, fifty years after the founding of the *Flying Saucer Review*, said:

> As I have matured I have looked for explanations for what we were reporting, the question of dimension and time in all this. Also I have thought of them just passing through our dimension rather than specifically coming here for any purpose. I make the analogy of sitting in a car sideways rather than straight ahead. As another car passes you, you see something pass through your time dimension. As it speeds on, it leaves your position in space and we have no control over its passing. I believe the answer to everything exists if you have the right questions.

The editorship of *Flying Saucer Review* passed to Brinsley Le Poer Trench, who remained in the post from September 1956 to 1959. Under his watch, the magazine developed a reputation for being an uncritical periodical. In 1957, a second founder disappeared from the roster.

Denis Montgomery, one of the chief catalysts in the birth of the magazine, had taken on the administrative role of Company Secretary. His original plans to create a library or institute for the study of UFOs never materialised due to a lack of funds. In 1957, his commercial career took him back to Africa and for the next six years he was an area petroleum sales manager and manager for the rubber purchasing and processing department for the United Africa Company in Nigeria. Returning to South Africa he worked as a stock distribution and production planning controller for Southern Africa, later working as a management consultant in South Africa, as commercial director for an eco-tourism project in Mozambique and for engineering and textile manufacturing companies in Brazil and England.

Brinsley Le Poer Trench's departure in 1959 occurred with little fanfare and with no reasons given. There is some uncertainty to the date of Trench's leaving and Waveney Girvan's taking on the task of editing. Charles Bowen, writing on the occasion of the magazine's tenth anniversary (*FSR* v.10 no.6, Nov/Dec 1964), recalled, "I had long been an admirer of Waverney's work, particularly after he had taken over as Editor of the Review in 1959." In the paper's 25th anniversary issue (v.26 no.1, June 1980), he specifies September 1959. Eileen Buckle (who, some nine years later, became heavily-involved in the production of the magazine) believes the change came in 1960. "From the back issues I can tell you [going by details on the masthead] that Waveney took over the reins either from the March/April 1960 issue or the July/August 1960 issue (these two crucial issues are missing from my files) but his name appears as editor in the Sep/Oct 1960 issue."

It would make sense that Trench's attentions were distracted during the period 1959-60, as his first book, *The Sky People*, was published in 1960. Confusion reigns (albeit mildly). If Bowen's date of "1959" is correct, did it really take a further year for anyone to notice that the masthead had been wrong for the previous four or five issues?

However, having said that, 1959 had been a pretty difficult year for many connected to the publishing industry generally. In addition to many companies having been bought out, masticated and swallowed whole by some of the larger conglomerates, during May and June, there had been a disastrous six-week-long national print strike that had had the throttling effect of killing off so many periodicals that had been struggling-financially anyway. The *Flying Saucer Review* survived by issuing an emergency roneoed edition

But on a happier note, in a report emanating from the other side of the world, things appeared to be fairing far rosier. A missionary and many aboriginal natives had seen several UFOs on the 26th of June with one seemingly in the throes of being repaired by four human-like occupants. The report went on to say that the witnesses and the aliens had waved to each other.

# CHAPTER EIGHT: GIRVAN'S DARK DAYS

In the early 1960s, Charles Bowen – the cashier based at the South African Embassy – was still balancing his account's books. With his attention having been drawn to its existence by articles offered in the "national dailies", he too had subscribed and had been an avid reader of the *Flying Saucer Review* right from its very beginning. For good reason, Bowen now comes back into the story, and although neither a date nor a place is given, the following quote speaks of a time when Girvan must have already taken over the editorship of FSR:

> It was just by chance that I met Waveney Girvan. I remember how I had been discussing some small official matter with a colleague, when to my surprise I saw a copy of the *Flying Saucer Review* among some papers on his desk Surprise indeed, for that particular gentleman was a sceptic if ever there was one! 'When he learned that I had been a regular reader of the *Review* since 1955, my colleague observed that it was high time I met the editor. My expression must have betrayed that I expected a leg-pull, for he hastened to add that the editor of the *Review* had at one time published a book for him.

"Small official matter" has the feel of a workplace discussion, and the colleague was almost certainly someone Bowen worked with at the South African Embassy. Waveney Girvan's publishing days had resulted in the publication of hundreds of books under a variety of imprints (Westaway Books, Carroll & Nicholson, T. Werner Laurie). But back to Bowen:

> He was as good as his word: Waveney accepted his invitation, and we spent two convivial hours discussing every aspect of the flying saucer mystery.
>  It was a wonderful evening for me, for I had long been an admirer of Waveney's work, particularly after he had taken over as Editor of the Review in 1959. When it was time to go, I was delighted to find that our guest and I had to catch the same train from Waterloo!

> That was a few years ago, and since that day we travelled together much of the time . . . until August this year.

The above was written by Charles Bowen following the premature death of Waveney Girvan at the age of 56. Bowen speaks of Girvan as having been "a chartered accountant, a distinguished author, a successful publisher, founder and chairman of the West Country Writers' Association, literary executor to the estate of Eden Phillpotts, an inventor, an latterly, a top executive of a great publishing house". It is a relatively easy task to establish the truth of all of these statements, as indeed we did for the most in an earlier chapter. His credits as an inventor include a series of patents for improved methods of united the ends of metal band straps and making pipe joints.

Since 1952, Girvan had been chief editor for T Werner Laurie at No 1, Doughty Street, London W.C.1. It is not known just when he left Laurie, but they were known as a publisher of *risqué* titles and, in May 1954, T. Werner Laurie, the printer Northumberland press and author Mrs. Kathryn Dyson-Taylor all pleaded guilty to publishing an obscene book, *Julia*.

Werner Laurie's former editor and director George Greenfield and Alan Palmer Caldicott, director of the printers, pleaded not guilty (although he changed his plea on one summons in court). Publisher, printer, authoress Taylor and managing director Caldicott were all fined; Greenfield was found guilty on one summons and discharged absolutely on payment of five guineas costs.

In June 1955, there was more embarrassment for T. Werner Laurie when Alfonso Barda, a Tripoli businessman was able to prove that he had been libelled in the book *Guns, Drugs and Deserters*, published in 1954. Barda also successfully sued Odhams over an article that had appeared in *John Bull*.

Soon after, in February 1957, the publishing firm was bought out by Max Reinhardt Ltd., which had also recently acquired John Lane and The Bodley Head in December 1956. The three imprints were to be retained but the firms would be run as one with the same editorial, production, sales and publicity departments, which would result in considerable economies. It seems likely that this was the time when Waveney Girvan parted company with T. Werner Laurie.

There is a possibility that Girvan joined Odhams Press at around the same time that he took over the editorship of *FSR*. In the late 1950s, Girvan had moved to The Oast House, Dogmersfield, Basingstoke, Hampshire, but was still commuting into London in the early 1960s, as recalled by Charles Bowen.

A series of take-overs had occurred in 1959 which saw the Amalgamated Press sold to Daily Mirror Newspapers Ltd. and renamed Fleetway Publications; meanwhile both Hulton Press and George Newnes sold to Odhams Press, who were then taken over by Fleetway in 1961. This brought a number of famous comics—*Eagle, Girl, Swift* and *Robin*—into the ownership of the company who published their rivals, *Lion, Tiger, School Friend, Girls' Crystal, Playhour* and dozens of others. These were nervous times for the employees of the Juvenile Publications department, who were unsure what effect these take-overs would have on the titles they worked on and whether titles and offices would be merged to save costs.

Into this environment came Waveney Girvan. He had been allocated a small, obscure office to the rear of one being occupied by the editorial staff of *Girl* magazine. In that room were Chief Sub-Editor Shirley Dean, Sub-Editors Anne Littlefield and Linda Wheway, and Designer Roger Perry. Girvan's comings and goings from that back room had – for at least a year – been acknowledged with little more than a "Good morning" or a "Good night", but due to his quiet unobtrusive manner, his austere attire of black jacket, striped trousers of narrow grey and black, neatly rolled umbrella and a bowler hat, plus the fact that he often only appeared once or twice a week. As Roger Perry recalled: "He was not someone who one really wanted to know. It was assumed that he had something to do with accountancy. It was only when Juvenile Publications was forcibly relocated to the Old Daily Herald building in Longacre in November 1963 – Girvan having been relocated along with everyone else – that he began to be accepted as not being a spy from the dreaded *Daily Mirror* camp after all."

This re-location to Longacre admirably suited Charles Bowen, for not only was it now little more than a ten-minute walk away from his place of work, but also the three people he most wanted to see – Albert Cosser (Sub-editor of *Boys' World*), Dan Lloyd (Chief Sub-Editor of *Eagle*) and Waveney Girvan (Editor of *Flying Saucer Review*) – all had offices just yards away from each other. It was particularly perfect as Bowen was in the process of providing the recently-launched *Boys' World* comic with a series of sporting scripts.

He was writing a series called Sports Star Specials of which 37 episodes had centred around sporting heroes from football to cricket and from rugby to speedway such as Stanley Matthews, Jimmy Greaves, Freddie Truman, Colin Cowdrey, Jack Brabham and Bobby Moore. These articles were innovative insofar that the illustrated biographies were in continuity-strip form with the occasional photograph being thrown in – meaning that the artists chosen had to be capable of capturing the individual's likeness. Paul Trevillion (who later went on to fame as the artist who illustrated 'You Are the Ref') drew 34 of these episodes while Roland Davies and Harry Lindfield illustrated the other three.

While calling in to deliver the latest script, it would have been a simple matter of walking just four offices down the corridor to call in and pass the time of day with Girvan. But this had been almost an unnecessary exercise, as Bowen's obituary on Girvan explains:

> For me, the drudgery of London commuting vanished from the time I met Waveney Girvan. Ufology was certainly not our only topic of conversation, but at times it was the most exciting one. And amusing too when we considered the evasive antics of authority, and the stuffiness of sceptics! Well I remember the "kick" we had from Aimé Michel's letter and article about Vauriat, and the discovery of global orthoteny. I remember too how proud Waveney was of the new-look cover which appeared on the May-June issue of 1963, an issue which he considered one of the best ever – until others even better came along! Perhaps the most exciting time of all was at the height of the Charlton crater affair, which culminated in Waveney's debunking of "Dr." Randall. I'll always treasure the memories of those evenings in the train.

Girvan himself recalled 1960, 1961 and 1962 as "particularly dark".

> As far as general interest was concerned, the saucers might as well have disappeared from our skies. While it

was true that local reports kept coming in, the public got it into their heads that the subject was indeed nonsensical and that it was nothing more than an out-of-date newspaper stunt. Thanks to the Charlton Crater mystery of 1963, and despite officialdom's attempt (unsuccessful as it happened) to write it off in terms of a meteorite, and other efforts made by exhibitionists to jump on the bandwagon, the public began to resume an interest in UFOs. The particular issue in which the *Review* dealt with the Charlton Crater quickly sold out although we had ordered a larger than usual number of copies. This brought in a healthy increase in readership. There is really only one thing that brings us a larger circulation and that is publicity in the press. How can one expect large numbers of new readers if the general public has been brainwashed into believing that saucers do not exist?

Aimé Michel was a former teacher and radio journalist, born in St. Vincent-les-Forts in 1919 to a modest farming family. He had suffered from childhood polio which left him with lifelong physical effects, his lower limbs being stunted, although he overcame his handicap to undertake difficult mountain climbs during his youth. Michel published two early books on flying saucers, amongst the first in France, entitled *Lueurs sur les soucoupes volantes* (1954) and *Mystérieux objects célestes* (1958).

Michel's chief claim to fame was the development of *orthoténie*, a theory that flying saucers flew in straight lines and that sightings of UFOs were aligned along paths that were large circles centred on the earth. Bowen's first article on UFOs speculated that the reason why we were seeing Aimé Michel's orthoteny lines was that, in order to time-travel, UFOs could only use certain physical routes. Bowen went on to say that the minimalist true communication by UFOnauts was to avoid "changing the future" by imparting usable information, this being his variation of the "grandfather paradox". (In the "grandfather paradox", a time-traveller goes back to a time before his grandfather married. The time-traveller kills his grandfather and, therefore, his father is never born; nor is the time-traveller. But if he was never born, he is unable to travel through time to kill his grandfather... which means his grandfather survived, the time-traveller was born and is able to travel back in time to kill his grandfather... and so on in an endless loop.)

When Girvan and the entire Juvenile Publications staff moved to Longacre in November 1963, he brought with him a secretary, Margaret ("Madge") Harman. For reasons not explained, Madge was given desk space in an office already occupied by *Eagle*'s Chief Sub-Editor Dan Lloyd and *Eagle* designer Brian (Benny) Green. Madge Harman was a closet 'psychic'.

An example of her extraordinary sixth sense came to light when one of Lloyd's drinking pals called into the office late one morning to find out if Dan was free for lunch. In those days, Lloyd would regularly meet with five friends from all walks of life; on this occasion, Lloyd introduced Harman to his flatmate Peter Henderson, and as they shook hands, Harman had suddenly gone quiet and in a disheartened voice had murmured: "Oh dear, you've had some bad news this morning... I'm so sorry."

Lloyd had no idea what she was talking about; shortly after, Henderson admitted that, just that morning, he had received a letter from his fiancée in Paris with news that she was breaking off their engagement. The letter had been tucked away in Henderson's inside jacket pocket.

It was during those early months at Longacre that a second strange occurrence took place.

Through a mixture of visits by Charles Bowen and the flow of conversations and information between the secretary and her boss, Dan Lloyd's interest in the paranormal was steadily rising. Lloyd not only become well-acquainted with the editor of *Flying Saucer Review* but, when he went on holiday, he took with him Girvan's book *Flying Saucers and Common Sense*, written nine years earlier.

Part way through – in chapter four – Lloyd was suddenly brought up with a start; that chapter included a personal letter written by Earl Mountbatten in 1950 and sent to the editor of the *Sunday Dispatch*. Girvan commented that this letter had followed an earlier article concerning a wave of UFO sightings in America, particularly of one seen in the town of Orangeburg. The letter said:

> These extraordinary things have now been seen in almost every part of the world – Scandinavia, North

America, South America, Central Europe, etc. Reports are always appearing and the newspapers generally try to ridicule them. As a result it is difficult for any seriously interested person to find out very much about them. I should therefore like to congratulate you on having had both the intelligence (and, incidentally, the courage) to print the first serious helpful article which I have read on the Flying Saucers. I have read most other accounts up to date, and can candidly say yours interested me the most.

Lloyd could hardly wait to return to his place of work so that he could confirm this story—because it was to Lloyd, who, as a 19-year-old stationed aboard HMS *Liverpool*, that Mountbatten had dictated the letter.

Astounded, Girvan bore Lloyd off to his club near Whitehall where, Lloyd found himself obliged to make a hasty, impromptu talk in front of a large gathering of dedicated followers and believers, verifying Girvan's claim over Mountbatten's interest in the flying saucer question.

Another of Girvan's unusual traits – apart from having psychic abilities – was a talent to "invent" things by dreaming about them; on waking the next morning, he would set about bringing his dreamt invention to life. It was due to one of these dreamt inventions that Lloyd was encouraged to introduce Girvan to Roger Perry.

Perry, whose office was just two doors down the corridor from where Lloyd worked, had been *Girl* magazine's designer; he was also an expert in photography and cinematography.

Girvan's latest invention was a method to project perfect 3D pictures onto a screen without having to use specially-made three-dimensional glasses. To prove his theory, Girvan had purchased two 35 mm slide projectors and a ViewMaster reel – this latter item consisting of a thin, circular cardboard disk that had seven stereoscopic pictures. The one Girvan had chosen had scenes from Walt Disney's version of *Alice in Wonderland*.

The procedure was simple enough. The two projectors were positioned side-by-side and close enough so that a spinning disc could be positioned in front of the two lenses. The circular disc had been fashioned with part of its surface missing so that as it spun, it prevented the light-beam of either one projector or the other from reaching the screen. The system worked perfectly ... but unfortunately, to create the three-dimensional illusion, the precise speed of the spinning disc had to be 17 revolutions per second and this hadn't tied in with either the standard 24 frames per second (as used in the projection of professional cinema film) or the 25 frames per second as used in transmitting television pictures – to fit in with the UK's standard frequency of 50 cycles per second where each frame is scanned and transmitted twice.

During July and August – before going on holiday – Perry had had several in-depth discussions on how to construct a "Maltese Cross" gear mechanism (also known as the Geneva Drive) – a device commonly used in advancing movie film in professional cinema projectors. His thoughts were that by using such a device, the alternate frames (representing first the left eye and then the right eye) could be captured by a single movie camera but one that had two lenses two-and-a-half-inches apart (thus maintaining the stereoscopy effect). The result would be a single length of movie film and it could be shown on a single film projector... it was the awkward 17-frames per second that had needed to be solved.

Following Perry's two-week break during September, several weeks passed before he came to the conclusion that he hadn't seen Waveney for quite some time – but then, often days would pass when Girvan hadn't appeared in his office anyway. It was Bert Fielder – the studio's in-house artist – to whom Perry had mentioned this observation when Fielder had replied: "Oh didn't you know? He died some weeks back – probably while you were still on holiday."

Charles Bowen recalled events over the summer thus:

> Last August it became increasingly apparent that Waveney was a sick man. When I returned from holiday last September, his seat in the train was empty: the journey was strangely quiet and lonely. I shall always treasure the memories of those evenings in the train.

Perhaps Girvan had already known that his end was near, for whenever Harman had gone into his office, not only did he hide his hands from her view by placing them onto his lap under the desk, but on passing something over to her, he never allowed Harman ever to have any physical contact with him.

> I thought he was exhausted by the way he had thrown himself wholeheartedly into his work, his other projects, and the editing of the *Review* – a single-handed marathon for the best part of five years! – but that turned out to be wishful thinking. For all who knew and loved Waveney Girvan, the world seemed an empty place on the morning of the 22nd October, 1964.

He died at The Royal Hampshire County Hospital, Winchester, aged 56. He was survived by his wife Barbara Newman Girvan (*née* Cann), whom he married in Newton Abbot, Devon, in 1936. They had a son, Ian A. Girvan, born in 1938, who later co-authored a number of book with Margaret Royal, including *True Stories of the Ghosts of Bath* (1974), *Local Ghosts: True Stories, Odd Happenings* (1976) *Bristol Ghosts and their Neighbours* (1977).

Charles Bowen recalled Girvan in a *FSR* obituary (v.10 no.6, Nov-Dec 1964)

> Waveney was wonderful company: an extremely intelligent man with a restless, inquiring mind; a man of infinite charm and sparkling wit, yet relentless in the pursuit of truth; a gentle man, not lacking in patience, yet impatient of bumbledom and mediocrity where better could be expected...

# CHAPTER NINE: BOWEN'S BRIGHTER FUTURE

With that same issue, Charles Bowen assumed the role of acting editor of the paper and was subsequently confirmed as editor. Waveney Girvan's secretary Madge Harman was not backwards in announcing that she favoured the appointment of Reginald Dutta as *Flying Saucer Review's* fourth editor. With Bowen's confirmed appointment, she decided to have nothing more to do with *FSR*.

In later years – and in private – Bowen divulged that he had nicknamed Reginald Dutta "Dutta the Nutter" because of his airy-fairy stance. Reginald Sirdar Mohammed Dutta was born in Lahore, India, on 11 July 1914, the son of Lall M. Dutta and his English wife, Marguerite M. E. Berghe, who were married in London in 1913. Dutta had spent his childhood in India and England before Marguerite returned to the UK permanently in around 1924 along with her two children, Reginald and Florence, born in 1921. A second sister died young in an accident.

The family lived in Upper Addison Gardens, Kensington, and Dutta became recognised as an aquarist – an expert in fish – on which subject he wrote numerous books, beginning with *The Right Way to Keep Pet Fish* in 1951. His main job was running Fish Tanks Ltd. at 49 Blandford Street, London W.1. Dutta was married to Olive Dorothy Parton-Old in 1944, but continued to live with his mother and sister for many years.

Known to his friends as Rex, Dutta was involved in a motorcycle accident during the early British expedition into France during WWII, which resulted in having his left leg amputated above the knee before being evacuated from Dunkirk.

Dutta, his wife and his mother became interested in Theosophy and active in the Theosophical Society; Rex started a class in The Secret Doctrine in the late 1950s and eventually he helped set up the newsletter *Viewpoint Aquarious* in 1972, dedicated to flying saucers, Theosophy, yoga and healing. He died in August 1989.

Little more was heard of Madge Harman, apart from a letter she wrote for publication in *FSR* as a tribute to Girvan:

Sir, Upon looking through Waveney Girvan's personal file on Flying Saucers, I came across something that reminded me of an incident which happened last summer. Somehow, I don't feel entitled to keep it to myself.

    Mr Girvan was standing by his desk, reading something which had just arrived from a contributor, I believe. Without a word, he turned and handed it to me. He stood very still watching me read, and raised his eyebrows in that quizzical way of his when I had finished. I was greatly moved by the verses, and said so adding that I thought them wonderful.

    "Yes," he said. "That's what I feel. It could be the answer, couldn't it?"

    He read the verses again, and they seemed to have great significance for him. He asked me to look the poet up and type it out, which I did. It is by J. Addington Symonds (1840–93).

> These things shall be! A loftier race
> Than e'er the world hath known, shall rise
> With flame of freedom in their souls,
> And light of science in their eyes.
>
> They shall be pure from fraud, and know
> The names of priest and king no more;
> For them no placeman's hand shall hold
> The balances of peace and war.
>
> They shall be gentle, brave and strong,
> To spill no drop of blood, but dare
> All that may plant man's lordship firm
> On earth and fire and sea and air.
>
> Nation with nation, land with land,
> Unarmed shall live as comrades free;
> In every heart and brain shall throb
> The pulse of one fraternity.
>
> They shall be simple in their homes
> And splendid in their public ways,

> Filling the mansions of the state
> With music and with hymns of praise.
>
> In aisles majestic, hails of pride,
> Groves, gardens, baths, and galleries,
> Manhood and youth and age shall meet
> To grow by converse inly wise.
>
> Woman shall be man's mate and peer,
> In all things strong and fair and good.
>
> I can only say that the words "Gentle, brave and strong" apply to no man more than to Waveney Girvan, and the poem written so many years ago, breathes ideals which were his. "Simple in their homes and splendid in the public ways." . . . that too.

With Dan Lloyd acting as assistant editor, Bowen had quickly and efficiently stepped into Girvan's shoes. Albeit a little late, the Nov/Dec issue of *Flying Saucer Review* came out without a significant break. In the Jan/Feb issue, Bowen explained that Girvan used to prepare his articles well in advance, and this was why his last written piece had appeared posthumously.

By the March/April 1965 issue of *Flying Saucer Review*, Charles Bowen's name was appearing under the title 'Editor', Dan Lloyd was shown as assistant editor and Gordon Creighton was a 'Consultant'. In that issue's editorial, Bowen apologised for the fact that subscribers had had to wait so long for the Nov/Dec 1964 issue. A postal strike was one of the reasons offered. Bowen continued:

> Soon afterwards there was the illness and subsequent death of our Editor, Waveney Girvan.
> Most of you must have read Mr. Girvan's last article Ten Years Old, which appeared in the November/December issue, so you will realize that the Review is managed solely by the Editor, with valuable and essential help from his production assistant, and from the lady who handles distribution. All this work is voluntary, or semi-voluntary, and is done in our spare time.

And so it was that Charles Bowen took over the editorship of *Flying Saucer Review* – which he presided over for the following eighteen years, editing 103 issues between 1964 to 1982. Bowen is regarded by Gordon Creighton (who would later succeed him to the post) as "assuredly our hardest-working and most severely harassed editor, for he managed all this while still performing his full-time ten-to-five job in the Finance Dept. of the South African Embassy in London."

It was not long after Bowen had taken control of *FSR* that strange events began to occur in and around the Wiltshire town of Warminster. Naturally *Flying Saucer Review* became more than just a little interested and had covered in detail accounts of poltergeist-type noises, fleeting lights in the night ... All this combined to become the remarkable story known as 'The Warminster Phenomenon' (*FSR*, v.11 no.4 July/August 1965). In no time at all, interest was shown by the *News of the World* and the *Daily Mirror*, with articles appearing as early as June; the *Daily Mirror* even splashed a photograph of what was claimed to be a flying saucer seen over Warminster across its centre pages in September.

The teaming of Charles Bowen as editor and Gordon Creighton as consultant proved to be a winning combination. Creighton showed time and again his prowess with linguistics and served as the translator for dozens of important non-English language case-reports in the decades that followed.

Mrs Jo Hugill had replaced Madge Harman. Because Bowen held a full-time job, Mrs Hugill was obliged to travel daily from her home in Beckenham, Kent, so that she might assist Bowen with the large flow of correspondence. There came a time towards the end of 1968 when she fell ill and needed to be hospitalized, leaving Bowen with a problem. During a hospital visit, Mrs Hugill asked her friend Eileen Buckle if she could temporarily help out while she was off sick. Buckle readily agreed and every weekday – just as Hugill had – she met with Bowen during his lunch hour to discuss the latest batch of *FSR* correspondence awaiting reply, which she would then take back home to work on. Before lunchtime ended, the two also had to collect the next pile of mail, which would be discussed the following day.

The *Flying Saucer Review*'s postal address was 21 Cecil Court, the address of Watkins Bookshop, tucked away in a small alley just off

Charing Cross Road. It was extremely convenient as it was just a few minutes' walk away from Bowen's place of work. A second address in Peckham regularly published in the magazine was that of a Mrs Spencer, who efficiently handled the to-ing and fro-ing of subscriptions.

Following her eventual discharge from hospital, Jo Hugill decided to retire, leaving Eileen Buckle "holding the baby". Her daily trips to the heart of London continued. Meanwhile, *FSR*'s assistant editor, Dan Lloyd, was shortly to lose his job on the famous *Eagle* comic, which was to merge with *Lion* in 1969. Dan met up with Bowen at South Africa House on occasions and it was there that he first met Miss Buckle.

The *Flying Saucer Review* was assembled on the dining-room table of Charles Bowen's West Byfleet home. Working at home also meant that Bowen could rope in his daughter, Pauline – a trained artist – to create many of the illustrations.

Meanwhile, Eileen Buckle moved from Beckenham and settled in an apartment in Church Street, Chelsea, one floor up from where Dan Lloyd lived. She was now becoming far more deeply involved; her role of typing letters had progressed to proofreading galleys, then to general editing and, finally, to the pasting up of pages. According to Buckle, there had been a fairly lengthy period when Pauline Bowen ended her involvement and a replacement artist by the name of Terry Collins took over for a while; when he, too, moved on, Eileen Buckle added producing illustrations to her lengthening list of tasks.

On 20 February 1971, an entirely new boys' comic was launched. *Countdown* was intended to have a more scientific appeal to boys inspired by the space race and the ongoing Apollo moon landings. With Roger Perry as art editor, Dan Lloyd was encouraged to become the magazine's science correspondent and it was through him that Charles Bowen was invited to supply a weekly series of single-page articles using material from the endless supply of UFO sightings he had on file.

The magazine (in its original form) ran for 58 issues, during which time Bowen supplied his articles competently, efficiently and on time.

Meanwhile, at *Flying Saucer Review*, assistant editor Dan Lloyd gradually faded from the pages of the paper during the 1970s due to his work as a sub-editor with Purnell and, later, on *TV Times*. With editor Bowen continuing his employment at South Africa House, the bulk of the work now fell to Eileen Buckle, who became increasingly involved to the point where she was almost running the magazine single-handed. Although she was meeting with Bowen each day, she was taking on more of the workload and responsibility. On top of this, she also had to help with mailing out printed copies when required following the retirement of Mrs Spencer. On 28 March 1980, his 49th birthday, Dan Lloyd married Eileen Buckle.

Soon after, there was a change in the arrangements at *Flying Saucer Review*. "Charles was Editor of *FSR* until the Jan/Feb 1982 issue," says Eileen Lloyd. "The masthead of the March/April 1982 issue changed, with Gordon [Creighton] named as Editor, and Charles Bowen as the 'Consultant'; no reason for this switch-round was mentioned in either of those two issues.

"I know Charles's health was deteriorating in the early eighties. I happened to bump into him on Waterloo Station once, where he told me that amongst other things he had developed problems with his eyesight (tunnel vision, I think he said). On one occasion Gordon rang me up to ask if I would take on the editorship, but I was living in a very small flat and had no room there for running such an operation, and very little spare time (I was a freelance editor). I had to say 'no'. Gordon subsequently – perhaps a little reluctantly – took the job on himself and was editor right up to the time of his death on 16 July 2003, aged 95."

Bowen himself recalled his time as editor thus (*FSR* v.20 no.5, 1974):

> When writing a few words at the end of my first five years stint as Editor, I believe I made a remark to the effect that the first five years are always the worst. And, of course, I was completely wrong about that, for what I can remember of them they weren't a patch on the second five years! Even so those five years were well worthwhile in terms of results achieved, and the volume of work published, which far exceeded that of the first five years.
> 
> With another anniversary in the offing – the completion of twenty years of *FSR* – it will be better to leave any observations about achievements until then.

Bowen had seen the paper through postal strikes, power crises, paper shortages, the 3-day weeks, losing the Cecil Court address and other problems, including rumours of his own resignation.

With Bowen retiring due to ill-health in 1982, he was succeeded by the more out-spoken and boisterous Gordon Creighton. Creighton, influenced by various conspiracy theories, alienated many in the UFO establishment who no longer considered the *Flying Saucer Review* as being the unbiased serious UFO organ that it once was. John Rimmer, writing in *Magonia* in 1983 said:

> Most of the articles in this latest issue [v.28 no.3] seem to be promoting a conspiracy theory of ufology. One asks Are UFO Reports Subject in Britain to the D-Notice System and the Official Secrets Act? This tries to suggest that the Government is taking great pains to suppress the dissemination and collation of UFO reports. A nameless informant is quoted at length, only to come to the conclusion that he cannot actually remember whether or not a D-Notice was ever issued over a UFO report! In fact it would be most remarkable if some UFO reports were not subject to the Official Secrets Act, such is the scope of this Act, especially reports made by military personnel or near military installations. Being covered by the Official Secrets Act does not mean that a topic is particularly important, as FSR (and many other ufologists) seem to think (in fact the present writer had to sign the Official Secrets Act when he worked in a menial capacity in a firm which printed Government forms).

Its pages, concluded Rimmer, were becoming riddled with bizarre claims and allegations; serious conclusions were being replaced by baseless innuendo.

"Charles [Bowen] was in my opinion somewhat timid, just as Dr. J. Allen Hynek was, and often seemed afraid to defend his corner vigorously against the sceptics and the critics," Gordon Creighton said . "Had he stood his ground more firmly, on several accounts, I feel sure that we might have had a much greater readership today."

Editor Bowen's decision three years earlier (1968) to remove the bold name FLYING SAUCER REVIEW from our cover and to replace it by a meaningless logo was a disastrously foolish step, as I shall show. (I wonder what demon induced him to do that.)

For almost thirty years, after my long spell of duty in foreign parts, I always worked in London and I commuted daily from my home in Hertfordshire. For the first decade or so, to a certain special department in Whitehall and then, after that, to an office inside the building of the Royal Geographical Society in Kensington, where—while still employed by the Ministry of Defence—I was concerned with maps in various East European, Middle Eastern, and Far Eastern languages.

And during all those years that I travelled daily to London, I always made a special point of carrying and reading FSR in the train up to Baker Street and then on the Underground Line to Westminster or, later, to Kensington. And it must have happened on at least a dozen occasions that complete strangers would step across the gangway to me and say: "*Flying Saucer Review!* Where can I get that?".

On one particularly amusing occasion, just before I got out of the train in the Whitehall area, I noticed opposite me a high-ranking officer in Royal Air Force uniform, sitting beside, and talking with, a man in civilian clothes whom I knew to have a big job in the Ministry of Defence. Ten minutes later, as I was going up the steps of my Ministry, I found that they were both just in front of me, and I heard one of them say to the other: "Fantastic! Did you see that chap on the train who was reading a Russian astronomical journal and *Flying Saucer Review*?"

In 1983, the former diplomat and intelligence officer related an intriguing sequel to a talk that he had given to the House of Lords All-Party UFO Study Group in the November. He happened to broach the subject with a complete stranger whom he met on the train journey home. According to Timothy Good [http://www.nicap.org/reports/541004essex_good.htm]:

The Salandin case was brought up in the course of conversation, and the stranger turned out to be a former member of 604 Squadron. Gordon told him that *FSR* had investigated and published the case in its first issue, and asked if by chance he had ever heard of the magazine. "Oh, yes!" he replied. "We knew all about *Flying Saucer Review*. You were the people that we were always warned that we must keep away from."

Charles Arthur Bowen, author, editor and accountant died on 14 October 1987 aged 69. William Gordon Creighton, diplomat, civil servant and editor died on 16 July 2003, aged 95. The *Flying Saucer Review* continues today and can be subscribed to at the Flying Saucer Review website [http://www.fsr.org.uk/].

Printed in Great Britain
by Amazon